THE POWER OF WORDS

*250 inspirational quotes of great
minds that turned my life around*

AYO JIMMY

Author: Ayo Jimmy

Title: The Power of Words

Printed Edition Hardcopy ISBN-978-1-9997685-0-8

Printed Edition Paperback ISBN

Kindle Edition ISBN

Category: Personal Development/Self Help/Personal Growth/General.

Publisher: MIH Publishing

276 Welcombe Avenue Swindon

Wiltshire

SN32QN

United Kingdom

Printed and bound in United Kingdom

Introduction

The biggest difference between those who are successful in achieving their dreams and those who are not is the belief they associate with their dreams. Having control over our beliefs is one of the most powerful things we can ever do to live life on our own terms. Our feelings, attitudes and behaviour all grow from our belief. Our life shrinks and expands in proportion to our belief in what we think we can or we can't do. It is our belief that makes us who we are and enhances our actions. Our belief is one of the most powerful tools that can help shape our destiny if we enact its power. Whatever your belief system is rooted in, your ability to rekindle it at all times matters. We can continuously reenergise our belief and hope of transforming our future for good by inculcating positive words of wisdom, which will enhance a positive mindset and courageous thoughts.

The power of words is showcased with alluring quotes, which will help you amplify your belief and transform your thoughts. The riveting, profound words in this book will enable you to turn daily challenges into stepping stones for achievement. You will be empowered with wisdom that will steer you from negative thinking and help you face every adversity with indubitable faith. The power of words will inspire you to use the circumstances that you think are setbacks as comebacks for your greatness.

The incredible quotes by great minds in this book have wonderful insights that will not only assist in shaping your perception about life but will also intensify your ability to overcome your limitations. These words will enable you to grow as a person and compel you to reach your maximum potential without any element of fear.

The best way to extract the nuggets from this book is read at least three quotes daily. Whether we like it or not, negativity is all around us and the only way to override it is to inspire our souls.

I hope every quote in this book resonates with your soul and instils in you the power to take positive action, as they did for me in times of adversity. I can guarantee that you will be blown away by the results you will achieve by meditating on these quotes daily.

Last, I want to say a big thanks to you for taking the time to purchase this thought-provoking book.

- *Talk to yourself more than you listen to yourself.* ~ Jon Gordon

- *The road to success is an untarred road called 'rejection', riddled with potholes called 'failures' and 'speedbumps' named 'broken hearts'. It will also be marred by traffic lights referred to as 'being broke'. If you can endure the speed limits you will arrive at your destination, called greatness.* ~ Ayo Jimmy

- *Never begin the day until it is finished on paper.* ~ Jim Rohn

- *The antidote for an abundant life is reading and hustle. Earn the respect and success through hard work.* ~ Ayo Jimmy

- *Life is 10% what happens to you and 90% how you react to it.* ~ Charles R Swindoll

- *Don't let someone else tell you what your time is worth. Find every opportunity within your tragedy and capitalise on it for your success. ~ Ayo Jimmy*

- *Success is a lousy teacher. It seduces smart people into thinking they can't lose. ~ Bill Gates*

- *Knowledge is a tool but its application is the new currency for wealth creation. ~ Ayo Jimmy*

- *Our greatest weakness lies in giving up. The most certain way to succeed is always to try just one more time. ~ Thomas A Edison*

- *Behind the mathematics of threats lies an opportunity. To find the opportunity you have to unveil the threat. ~ Ayo Jimmy*

- *The mathematician of life is encompassed by millions of questions. Be willing to find the answers by asking. ~ Ayo Jimmy*

- *Problems are not stop signs; they are guidelines. ~ Robert H Schuller*

- *Implementation of knowledge brings two essential things to human life: wealth and wisdom. ~ Ayo Jimmy*

-

- *If you want to conquer fear, don't sit at home and think about it. Go out and get busy. ~ Dale Carnegie*

- *The nugget of wisdom to solve any uncomfortable situation is hidden in books. Be open to new ways of learning. There is no productivity shortcut to success. ~ Ayo Jimmy*

- *Indecisiveness is mere thinking that is negated by decision making. ~ Ayo Jimmy*

- *What you get by achieving your goals is not as important as what you become by achieving your goals. ~ Zig Ziglar*

- *Finding a way to overcome timidity and cowardice by confronting the conflicts of life with a new sense of self-mastery will obliterate your mental picture of the unknown. ~ Ayo Jimmy*

- *The people who influence you are the people who believe in you. ~ Henry Drummond*

- *Have the will to succeed by conquering the paralysis of fear and failure. Set the seal of courage and determination in all your actions. ~ Ayo Jimmy*

- *Be super specific about who you want to become in life through what you do each day. Let your mind mirror your beliefs. ~ Ayo Jimmy*

- *You may not control all the events that happen to you, but you can decide not to be reduced by them. ~ Maya Angelou*

- *Mistakes don't kill but ignorance does; don't be afraid to make one. ~ Ayo Jimmy*

- *Perfection is not attainable, but if we chase perfection we can catch excellence. ~ Vince Lombardi*

- *Do not be afraid to make radical change if the opportunity presents itself. Liberate the forces of doubt within you. ~ Ayo Jimmy*

- *Courage is a priceless asset for those who are keen to transform their life. Find a passion that will become your all consuming desire. ~ Ayo Jimmy*

- *Change your thoughts and you change your world. ~ Norman Vincent Peale*

- *Knowledge is a product of unexpected failures. Fail your way to success. ~ Ayo Jimmy*

- *Avoid disempowering thoughts and perceptions about who you aspire to be. Find hidden opportunities in change. Life is full of challenges. ~ Ayo Jimmy*

- *The pessimist sees difficulty in every opportunity. The optimist sees the opportunity in every difficulty. ~ Winston Churchill*

- *Your ability to turn ideas into innovative reality will make you a legend among your peers; earn the respect of success through smart working. ~ Ayo Jimmy*

- *You learn more from failure than from success. Don't let it stop you. Failure builds character. ~ Unknown*

- *True wisdom lies in knowing when not to quit when you are chasing your dreams. You will beat all odds if you persist. ~ Ayo Jimmy*

- *Live your life as an exclamation rather than an explanation. ~ Isaac Newton*

- *Outstanding people have some things in common, such as discipline and determination to persist when the struggles get tougher. Be your own cheerleader. ~ Ayo Jimmy*

- *Yearning for more accomplishments is the philosophy of the great, mastered by the ambitious, practiced by the determined.* ~ Ayo Jimmy

- *Pride is an admission of weakness; it secretly fears all competition and dreads all rivals.* ~ Fulton Sheen

- *Creativity is a product of imperfection. Let your mistakes drive you to break new ground.* ~ Ayo Jimmy

- *If you do not have an agenda for your life you will be a part of someone else's agenda.* ~ Les Brown

- *See yourself in your mind and let your subconscious mind create the reality of who you want to become. Don't be at the mercy of other people's opinion when designing the best version of you.* ~ Ayo Jimmy

- *When you change your thoughts you change your perception and that changes your language. ~ Ayo Jimmy*

- *The major reason for setting a goal is for what it makes of you to accomplish it. What it makes of you will always be the far greater value than what you get. ~ Jim Rohn*

- *Getting empowered is a choice and we are the architect of its existence. ~ Ayo Jimmy*

- *If you are working on something exciting that you really care about, you don't have to be pushed. The vision pulls you. ~ Steve Jobs*

- *A renewed mindset propels action. ~ Ayo Jimmy*

- *People who are crazy enough to think they can change the world are the ones who do. ~ Rob Siltanen*

- *Creativity is an unspecified mistake that leads to unique innovative outcomes. Live outside your comfort zone by thinking without limitations. ~ Ayo Jimmy*

- *Strength does not come from winning. Your struggles develop your strengths. When you go through hardships and decide not to surrender, that is strength. ~ Arnold Schwarzenegger*

- *Courage and determination are inner attributes that cannot be taught but can be inspired. ~ Ayo Jimmy*

- *There are two ways of exerting one's strength: one is pushing down, the other is pulling up. ~ Booker T. Washington*

- *The rail of life is filled up with shackles, It's only the determined who can journey through it and turn the shackles to success.* ~ *Ayo Jimmy*

- *There are better starters than me but I'm a strong finisher.* ~ *Usain Bolt*

- *The hero in your story of life is you and the enemy is also you; which one you become depends on your mindset.* ~ *Ayo Jimmy*

- *You are always free to choose what you do first, what you do second, and what you do not do at all.* ~ *Brian Tracy*

- *Transformation is not a one-time recipe for greatness. It is a continuous process.* ~ *Ayo Jimmy*

- *The uneducated mind is likened to walking in the light with your eyes open but you can't see. Don't give yourself an excuse to be crippled by your own ignorance. ~ Ayo Jimmy*

- *Strength and growth come only through continuous effort and struggle. ~ Napoleon Hill*

- *Consistency creates improvement and improvement brings out the best in you. ~ Ayo Jimmy*

- *Let fear be a counsellor and not a jailer. ~ Tony Robbins*

- *There are two tragedies that can destroy a man's destiny. One is to admit failure; the other is to believe that you are a failure. Don't let the seed of negativity bury your vision. ~ Ayo Jimmy*

- *Strive not to be a success but rather to be of value.* ~ *Albert Einstein*

- *Don't live to wake up and find out that your vision has been achieved by someone who believes in its reality. Be the architect of your dreams.* ~ *Ayo Jimmy*

- *The past cannot be changed but the future is still in your power.* ~ *Hugh White*

- *Life happens to you, not for you. Suspend your disbelief about who you want to become.* ~ *Ayo Jimmy*

- *Work hard in silence; let your success be your noise.* ~ *Frank Ocean*

- *The principles that we adopt in life and in business shape our destiny and influence our decisions. ~ Ayo Jimmy*

- *Gratitude is the single most important ingredient to living a successful and fulfilled life. ~ Jack Canfield*

- *Emancipate yourself from negative perceptions. You are responsible for your own change, not anyone else. ~ Ayo Jimmy*

- *There will be obstacles. There will be doubters. There will be mistakes. But with hard work, there are no limits. ~ Michael Phelps*

- *Commitment to never-ending improvement is a concept that creates great innovations. Be your source of change. ~ Ayo Jimmy*

- *Failure is not an option but it is a lesson that we need to learn before we can unfold victory. Let failing be part of your life experience for greatness. ~ Ayo Jimmy*

- *We may encounter many defeats but we must not be defeated. ~ Maya Angelou*

- *Your 'WHY' will build your innate desire for greatness if you emotionalise it with the willingness to achieve undoubtable results. ~ Ayo Jimmy*

- *You are just about as happy as you decide to be. Make up your mind to be a cheerful, optimistic person. ~ Brian Tracy*

- *When the decision you have made in life's situation takes you on a different pathway, enjoy the journey because the outcomes of this decision may be the solution to upcoming problems. ~ Ayo Jimmy*

- *You don't get successful by luck; you get successful by learning. ~ Ayo Jimmy*

- *Our greatest weakness lies in giving up. The most certain way to succeed is to try just one more time. ~ Thomas Edison*

- *Time is precious but value is expensive. Create value so that you don't have to work for time. ~ Ayo Jimmy*

- *Success is not so much what we have as it is what we are. ~ Jim Rohn*

- *Ideas plus inspiration equals transformation. ~ Ayo Jimmy*

- *Anger imprisons the positive side of man and makes him a slave to his circumstances. ~ Ayo Jimmy*

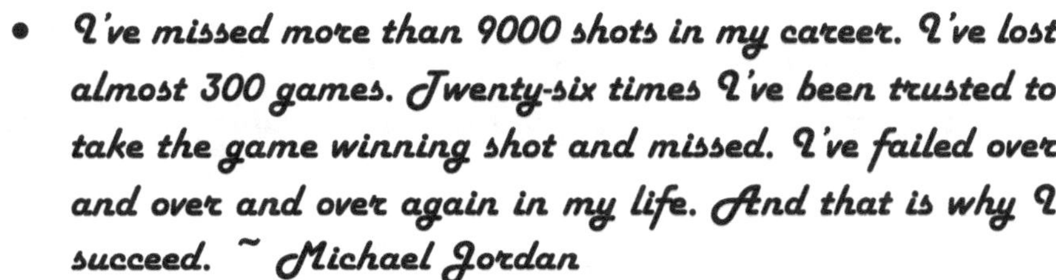

- *I've missed more than 9000 shots in my career. I've lost almost 300 games. Twenty-six times I've been trusted to take the game winning shot and missed. I've failed over and over and over again in my life. And that is why I succeed. ~ Michael Jordan*

- *Passion is an addiction that is intoxicating if you propel it with action. ~ Ayo Jimmy*

- *We become what we think about. ~ Earl Nightingale*

- *The possibility of failing in any event has nothing to do with the risk encountered during the journey. It has a lot to do with the perception that you have created toward taking action. ~ Ayo Jimmy*

- *Perfection is an excuse for not coming to play in the game of life. ~ Ayo Jimmy*

- *Our attitude at the beginning of a task will affect its outcome more than anything else. ~ John C. Maxwell*

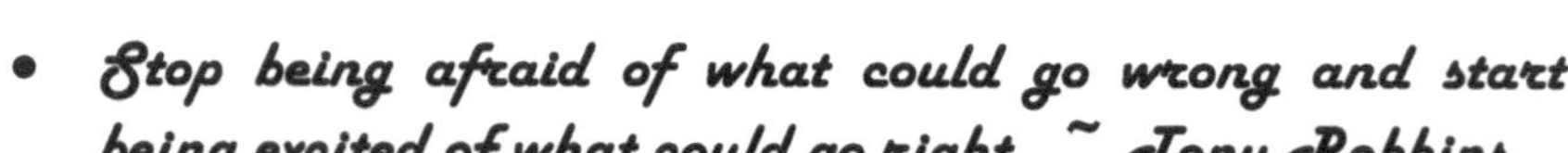

- *Stop being afraid of what could go wrong and start being excited of what could go right. ~ Tony Robbins*

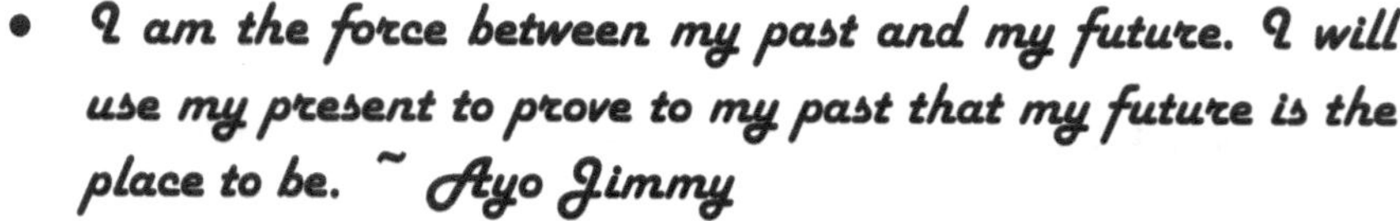

- *I am the force between my past and my future. I will use my present to prove to my past that my future is the place to be. ~ Ayo Jimmy*

- *You've got to get up every morning with determination if you're going to go to bed with satisfaction. ~ George Horace Lorimer*

- *Don't suffer fools gladly. Success is real if you believe in its achievement. ~ Ayo Jimmy*

- *Diligence is the heart of discipline. Action is the power that propels it. ~ Ayo Jimmy*

- *Twenty years from now you will be more disappointed by the things that you didn't do than by the ones you did do, so throw off the bowlines, sail away from safe harbour, catch the trade winds in your sails. Explore, Dream, Discover. ~ Mark Twain*

- *Don't let distraction distract you because you can turn your I CAN'T!! To I CAN!! ~ Ayo Jimmy*

- *It's not the mountain we conquer, but ourselves. ~ Edmund Hillary*

- *A fail is not a failure until you allow it to affect you. ~ Ayo Jimmy*

- *Don't be ignorant of your true identity by striving for things which will not lead you to your greatness; challenge the old beliefs in your subconscious mind. ~ Ayo Jimmy*

- *Your time is limited, so don't waste it living someone else's life. ~ Steve Jobs*

- *Fear is a fallacy that can prevent you from creating the reality of your future. Avoid overestimating risks and underestimating your ability to overcome them. ~ Ayo Jimmy*

- *I am not a product of my circumstances. I am a product of my decisions. ~ Stephen Covey*

- *Time management is an irreplaceable resource that will help you complete more tasks for less. ~ Ayo Jimmy*

- *Today's accomplishments were yesterday's impossibilities. ~ Robert H Schuller*

- *Luck favours the prepared; allocate your time so that it will have more positive impact. ~ Ayo Jimmy*

- *Setting goals is the first step in turning the invisible into the visible. ~ Tony Robbins*

- *Poverty is rooted in little or no access to mental development. Don't be lazy in learning. ~ Ayo Jimmy*

- *The will to win, the desire to succeed, the urge to reach your full potential: These are the keys that will unlock the door to personal excellence. ~ Confucius*

- *Pain and problems are by-products of progress; use them until they lead you to your prosperity. ~ Ayo Jimmy*

- *It's fine to celebrate success but it is more important to heed the lessons of failure. ~ Bill Gates*

- *Discipline is the real crux for success, stay hungry. ~ Ayo Jimmy*

- *Knowing is not enough; we must apply. Wishing is not enough; we must do. ~ Johann Wolfgang Von Goethe*

- *The best way to die for your dreams is to live a life worthy of them. ~ Ayo Jimmy*

- *Fear does not exist in reality except in the mind. Don't be so blinded with your perception of it that you cannot see the materialisation of your dreams. ~ Ayo Jimmy*

- *Creativity is intelligence having fun. ~ Albert Einstein*

- *Happiness is an emotion that emanates from the heart but it radiates from the soul. ~ Ayo Jimmy*

- *What you lack in talent can be made up with desire, hustle and giving 110% all the time. ~ Don Zimmer*

- *All actions fashioned by human beings started with thinking; think your way to success positively with actions. ~ Ayo Jimmy*

- *Poverty is not a necessity of nature. Change your perception about financial freedom and don't be ashamed to acquire wealth. ~ Ayo Jimmy*

- *Make up your mind that no matter what comes your way, no matter how difficult, no matter how unfair, you will do more than simply survive. You will thrive in spite of it. ~ Joel Osteen*

- *Determination can reshape your future for good. Use your extraordinary abilities to see the possibilities of your vision unfolding. ~ Ayo Jimmy*

- *Sometimes you don't realise your own strength until you come face to face with your greatest weakness. ~ Susan Gale*

- *Success is all about systems; work within it as it flows. ~ Ayo Jimmy*

- *A change is brought about because ordinary people do extraordinary things. ~ Barack Obama*

- *Your fear won't break you but your decision will. ~ Ayo Jimmy*

- *Our greatest glory is not in never failing, but in rising up every time we fail. ~ Ralph Waldo Emerson*

- *Every challenge is trials of life that are filtered by determination and dedication. ~ Ayo Jimmy*

- *When you are grateful, fear disappears and abundance appears. ~ Tony Robbins*

- *Life transformation is a game of passion and persistence. Learn your ways to success. ~ Ayo Jimmy*

- *Learn from the mistakes of others. You can never live long enough to make them all yourself. ~ Groucho Marx*

- *Success has neither mercy for laziness nor pity for procrastination. Don't be casual with your dreams. ~ Ayo Jimmy*

- *Every problem has a tag with an expiry date on it and every dream has a fulfilment date attached to it. ~ Ayo Jimmy*

- *Couldn't, shouldn't and wouldn't are your three greatest enemies standing between you and your achievements. ~ Ayo Jimmy*

- *It is hard to fail, but it is worse never to have tried to succeed. ~ Theodore Roosevelt*

- *When you turn your pain to passion it leads to profit. ~ Ayo Jimmy*

- *Knowing others is wisdom; knowing yourself is enlightenment. ~ Lao Tzu*

- *Make every challenge you face in life be the shotgun that will kick-start your race to unstoppable greatness. ~ Ayo Jimmy*

- *Getting your foot on the ladder of success is not that easy. Have unfaltering desire to succeed. ~ Ayo Jimmy*

- *If we know exactly where we're going, exactly how to get there, and exactly what we'll see along the way, we won't learn anything. ~ Scott Peck*

- *Our fear is the by-product of our decisions. You either deal with it or it overwhelms you. ~ Ayo Jimmy*

- *Our life is what our thoughts make it. ~ Marcus Aurelius*

- *Having unclear goals gives you the permission to create reasons and no results. ~ Ayo Jimmy*

- *Books are for people who see the reality in the imagination of others as education is the ray of hope for curious minds. ~ Ayo Jimmy*

- *True leaders don't create followers; they create more leaders. ~ Tony Robbins*

- *Everything that is invisible is real but you will have to imagine it before you can make it visible. ~ Ayo Jimmy*

- *When you are transitioning to a new season of life, the people and situations that no longer fit you will fall away. ~ Mandy Hale*

- *You can become a victor through your own struggles but don't become a victim of your failures. Learn from your mistakes. ~ Ayo Jimmy*

- *The battle for greatness can only lead to victory, if we fight against struggle and adversity on a daily basis. ~ Ayo Jimmy*

- *I'm not extraordinary. I'm simply an ordinary woman who chooses every day to make extraordinary decisions. ~ Lisa Nichols*

- *Where there is no belief, there is no breakthrough. ~ Ayo Jimmy*

- *I learned that courage was not the absence of fear, but the triumph over it. The brave man is not he who does not feel afraid, but he who conquers that fear. ~ Nelson Mandela*

- *Your dream is the imaginative signpost to your destiny. ~ Ayo Jimmy*

- *Our past cannot be erased but our future can be empowered. Gamble not with your future, act now. ~ Ayo Jimmy*

- *Life opens up opportunities to you, and you either take them or you stay afraid of taking them. ~ Jim Carrey*

- *Your future is determined by the choices you make, not the ones that are made for you. Be worthy of your greatness. ~ Ayo Jimmy*

- *Our job is not to figure out the how. The how will show up out of the commitment and the belief in the what. ~ Jack Canfield*

- *Fear is the root of all evil that kills the power of belief and action in you. Make tenacity and boldness your bosom friends. ~ Ayo Jimmy.*

- *It is not the most intelligent but the most determined who snatches victory from the jaws of defeat and failures. ~ Ayo Jimmy*

- *When your clarity meets your conviction and you apply action to the equation your world will begin to transform before your eyes. ~ Lisa Nichols*

- *Fit more into the day than others fit into a week; there is no progress without risks. ~ Ayo Jimmy*

- *The difference in living and feeling alive is using your fear as fuel to fly. ~ India Arie*

- *In life opportunities don't come looking for you and they will not arrive by special delivery. You have to go out there and hunt for them. ~ Ayo Jimmy*

- *Success brings a sense of meaning to life. Sacrifice every hour of your day for your unlimited greatness. ~ Ayo Jimmy*

- *Life is like riding a bicycle. To keep your balance, you must keep moving. ~ Albert Einstein*

- *Creativity is allowing yourself to make mistakes. Art is knowing which ones to keep. ~ Scott Adams*

- *Success has no colour or race. It only accepts those who are willing to break boundaries and become champions. ~ Ayo Jimmy*

- *Make no your vitamin; every no will bring you closer to a yes. ~ Les Brown*

- *Don't allow anyone define your level of capability for you. Turn mediocre spirit into passion and allow your self-reliance to drive you to your unlimited greatness. ~ Ayo Jimmy*

- *A dream becomes a goal when action is taken toward its achievement. ~ Bo Bennett*

- *Finding out the way things work is not a crime. It is a blessing that liberates the mind. Be inquisitive. ~ Ayo Jimmy*

- *Turn your wounds into wisdom. ~ Oprah Winfrey*

- *When you plug into your WHY, the HOW TO will arrive at your doorstep to help create the solution. ~ Ayo Jimmy*

- *We grow from pains and challenges. Set yourself up for success by making smarter choices in the present for a more secure future. ~ Ayo Jimmy*

- *Don't count the number of times you get knocked down. Get attached to the number of times you get back up. ~ Lisa Nichols*

- *Let the will to excel be the vital part of your decision. Have a resolute belief in who you want to become. ~ Ayo Jimmy*

- *I have no limits. I cannot be contained because I am the container. ~ Jim Carrey*

- *Don't squander your life away by helping others fulfil their vision. Identify why you are here and create greatness out of your destiny. ~ Ayo Jimmy*

- *Fear and disbelief are invisible emotions that can lead us astray and disempower our ability to fulfil our vision. ~ Ayo Jimmy*

- *The most successful people in life are the ones who ask questions. They're always learning. They're always growing. They're always pushing. ~ Robert Kiyosaki*

- *Your level of success will be determined by the level of help that you give to yourself. Be generous to whom you want to become. ~ Ayo Jimmy*

- *In the midst of hardship and struggles is where greatness is discovered. Don't quit. ~ Ayo Jimmy*

- *You don't have to be great to start, but you have to start to be great. ~ Zig Ziglar*

- *You have great potential locked up within you.*
  For you to truly discover yourself, you will have to continuously enlarge your safety net. ~ *Ayo Jimmy*

- *Don't be at mercy of your fear when designing your life. Have the natural curiosity to learn about your future in the face of unflinching struggles.* ~ *Ayo Jimmy*

- *I would rather be a hot mess of bold action, a make-it-happen-learn-on-the fly kind of person, than a perfectly organised coward.* ~ *Brendon Burchard*

- *Do you want to know who you are? Don't ask. Act! Action will delineate and define you.* ~ *Thomas Jefferson*

- *Let your vision break all protocol to the extent that you will be passionately determined to achieve it. Life is worth living.* ~ *Ayo Jimmy*

- *Unsuccessful people are the victims of their own philosophy. Take extant steps to achieve your purpose in life. ~ Ayo Jimmy*

- *If we paid attention to the obvious, we wouldn't end up with confusion. ~ Surya Nycole*

- *Impossibility becomes possible with dedication and persistence. ~ Ayo Jimmy*

- *If you want to be successful find someone who has achieved the results you want and copy what they do and you'll achieve the same results. ~ Tony Robbins*

- *Becoming successful is a choice and you are the architect of your greatness. ~ Ayo Jimmy*

- *The most dangerous man on earth is the man who is ready for change and will do everything to experience that transformation. ~ Ayo Jimmy*

- *Winners are not afraid of losing. But losers are. Failure is part of the process of success. People who avoid failure also avoid success. ~ Robert Kiyosaki*

- *We cannot teach people to be courageous but we can inspire them to be determined. ~ Ayo Jimmy*

- *Success is not measured by what you do compared to what others do, it is measured by what you do with the ability God gave you. ~ Zig Ziglar*

- *Change ignites friction; without change there is no transformation. ~ Ayo Jimmy*

- *The circumstances surrounding the events of life are not the game changer. It's your belief and will power that will turn the hand of time.* ~ *Ayo Jimmy*

- *Winners concentrate on winning; losers concentrate on getting by.* ~ *John C. Maxwell*

- *Make your mind an asset and not a liability. Your thought is a mirror of who you are.* ~ *Ayo Jimmy*

- *Who you become is what you create out of you.* ~ *Ayo Jimmy*

- *An attitude of positive expectation is the mark of the superior personality.* ~ *Brian Tracy*

- *I would rather learn and fail than to remain in a state of mediocrity. ~ Ayo Jimmy*

- *You are the prophet of your own greatness; evangelise it with action. ~ Ayo Jimmy*

- *God chooses what we go through; we choose how we go through it. ~ John C. Maxwell*

- *Education of the mind brings transformation that liberates and creates financial freedom. ~ Ayo Jimmy*

- *The more you seek security, the less of it you have. But the more you seek opportunity, the more likely it is that you will achieve the security that you desire. ~ Brian Tracy*

- *Do not desensitize yourself from the power of persistence. Use it as a road map to direct yourself to your unlimited treasures. ~ Ayo Jimmy*

- *Identify your problems but give your power and energy to solutions. ~ Tony Robbins*

- *When decision aligns with desire, action will emerge to create destiny and our dreams will be fulfilled. ~ Ayo Jimmy*

- *The size of your success is measured by the strength of your desire, the size of your dream, and how you handle disappointment along the way. ~ Robert Kiyosaki*

- *Persistence is a valuable virtue for success. ~ Ayo Jimmy*

- *Happiness is not something ready-made. It comes from your own actions.* ~ Dalai Lama

- *Make no mistake, the drawing board of your life needs planning and tactical sketching. You become what you create; don't wish your life way.* ~ Ayo Jimmy

- *Change is the middle door between the human race and their greatness; change is inevitable.* ~ Ayo Jimmy

- *Successful people are always looking for opportunities to help others. Unsuccessful people are asking 'what's in it for me.'* ~ Brian Tracy

- *Problems and pressure are the best prophets that propel prosperity.* ~ Ayo Jimmy

- *You are the only one who can fuel your passion and the momentum for that is governed by action. ~ Ayo Jimmy*

- *The twin killers of success are impatience and greed. ~ Jim Rohn*

- *Your intelligence will not create your abundant life and financial freedom but your 'why' will. ~ Ayo Jimmy*

- *Break the negative promise of impossibility that you made to yourself; you are not a spectator in the game of life. Find your path and life will yield to you. ~ Ayo Jimmy*

- *The foolish man seeks happiness in the distance; the wise man grows it under his feet. ~ James Oppenheim*

- *Don't push your future into the hands of the next generation. Use your potential and live your dream. ~ Ayo Jimmy*

- *The golden treasure of greatness lies inside each and every one of us; harvest it by unlocking the grip of fear. ~ Ayo Jimmy*

- *A breakthrough is a moment in time when the impossible becomes possible. ~ Tony Robbins*

- *The desire to strive for victory in the battlefield of life is a baton handed down to us by our ancestors who see success as a way of living and not a gift applicable to few. ~ Ayo Jimmy*

- *Any great achievement is preceded by many difficulties and many lessons; great achievements are not possible without them. ~ Brian Tracy*

- *You are equipped with everything it takes to take that inspired action to achieve your desired dream. You are unlimited; stop acting like you have limitations.* ~ *Ayo Jimmy*

- *You get in life what you have the courage to ask for.* ~ *Oprah Winfrey*

- *Let your innovation inspire your sense of purpose and sharpen your inner potential to lead you to unlimited greatness.* ~ *Ayo Jimmy.*

- *Changing your name will not change your destiny, but changing your philosophy of life will.* ~ *Ayo Jimmy.*

- *Invest wisely in your future development because it will make you a potential asset. Don't gamble with who you want to become.* ~ *Ayo Jimmy*

- *You have a choice and chance to create your heaven on earth. Never delay action until tomorrow; take the first step.* ~ *Ayo Jimmy*

- *Use your strength intelligently to propel your best effort for excellent achievement to prevail. Be desirous about who you want to become.* ~ *Ayo Jimmy*

- *The biggest adventure you can ever take is to live the life of your dreams.* ~ *Oprah Winfrey*

- *Don't be frightened by mistakes. Cherish them because you will learn from them.* ~ *Ayo Jimmy*

- *Action may not always bring happiness but there is no happiness without action.* ~ *Benjamin Disraeli*

- *The mathematics of breakthrough is Dream plus Drive plus Discipline equals Destiny. Use your decisions to drive your desire for greatness. ~ Ayo Jimmy*

- *Success is liking yourself, liking what you do, and liking how you do it. ~ Maya Angelou*

- *Limitation of self is an insanity that will lead you to total failure. Don't underestimate the power of your ability. ~ Ayo Jimmy*

- *Procrastination is the enemy of time; avoid deferring your future mission. ~ Ayo Jimmy*

- *Playing it safe is planning to fail. Risk it all for your vision. It is worth it. ~ Ayo Jimmy*

- *Every problem has a tag with an expiry date on it and every dream has a fulfilment date attached to it.* ~ Ayo Jimmy

- *Operate from your passion and not your pain.* ~ Ayo Jimmy

- *Vision is not a luxury. Its fulfilment is a necessity to those who believe in its reality. You are gifted with potential, make use of it.* ~ Ayo Jimmy

- *There is no security in life except for what lies inside of you. Put yourself at risk of experiencing abundant life that will secure your true identity.* ~ Ayo Jimmy

- *The performance that we give to a challenge will determine the outcome.* ~ Ayo Jimmy

- *Our vision is a channel of life that we must swim through to get to our greatness. ~ Ayo Jimmy*

- *Knowledge is the forerunner to success but its application brings success to reality. ~ Ayo Jimmy*

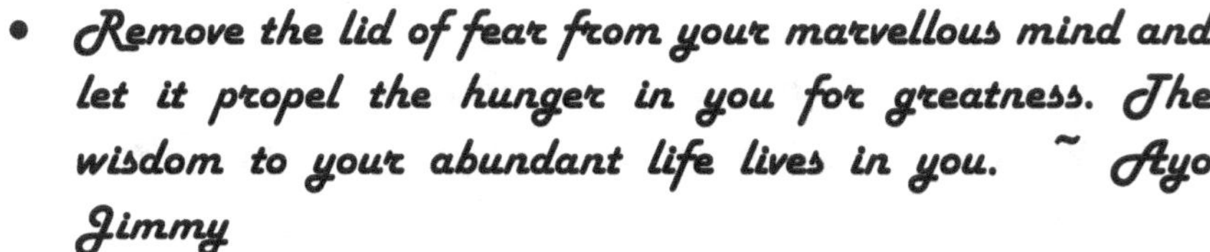

- *Remove the lid of fear from your marvellous mind and let it propel the hunger in you for greatness. The wisdom to your abundant life lives in you. ~ Ayo Jimmy*

- *To achieve anything in life, we must first overcome the idea of 'what will people think about me.' ~ Ayo Jimmy*

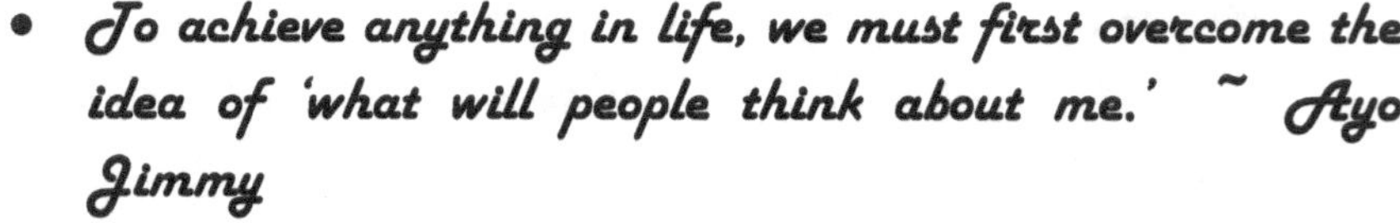

- *If life is not challenging you, the results will not change you. ~ Ayo Jimmy*

Now that you have completed **The Power of Words**, I believe you will be highly motivated to encourage others to follow in your footsteps and get hungry for greatness. To further enhance your personal development and continuous learning, please feel free to browse through copies of my other available books.

OTHER BOOKS FROM AYO JIMMY

These books will be available in the following formats: Hardcopy, Softcopy, Kindle, eBook and audio in various popular book platforms online, and you can also find out more information about the book on the website listed below.

http://www.inspirationandwisdomonline.com/
http://www.12virtuesoftheextraordinaries.com/